INSIDE THE TITANIC

Illustrated by Ken Marschall
Text by Hugh Brewster

A MADISON PRESS BOOK
Produced for
LITTLE, BROWN AND COMPANY
Boston   New York   Toronto   London

A LITTLE, BROWN BOOK
First published in Great Britain in 1998
by Little, Brown and Company (UK)

Produced by
Madison Press Books
40 Madison Avenue
Toronto
Ontario
Canada M5R 2S1

A CIP catalogue record for this book is available
from the British Library.

ISBN 0-316-64430-7

Design, Typography and Art Direction: Gordon Sibley Design Inc.
Editorial Director: Hugh Brewster
Project Editor: Mireille Majoor
Production Director: Susan Barrable
Production Coordinator: Sandra L. Hall
Color Separation: Colour Technologies
Printing and Binding: Artegrafica S.p.A.

INSIDE THE TITANIC
was produced by Madison Press Books, which is
under the direction of Albert E. Cummings

Little, Brown and Company (UK)
Brettenham House
Lancaster Place
London WC2E 7EN

Printed and bound in Italy

Sailing Day

Wednesday, April 10, 1912

"**C**ome along now, Frankie," his father called. "It's time to go on board." Frank Goldsmith took one last look up at the huge black hull of the *Titanic*. Far above him he could see people looking down over the railing on the top deck.

"Hurry up, boy, we're all waiting for you!" Frank turned and saw Alfred Rush standing next to him. Alfred put out his hand, but Frank ignored it. Frank was nine and thought he was too old to be led by the hand. And he was not about to be bossed by Alfred Rush, who was only fifteen.

The two boys joined Frank's parents, who were standing near a gangway that led to an open door in the side of the ship. With them was their friend and neighbor, Tom Theobald, who was also going to America on the *Titanic*. Frank's father and Mr. Theobald hoped to find work in Detroit, Michigan. Alfred Rush was also headed for Detroit to live with his older brother. Frank's parents had agreed to look after him during the voyage.

"All aboard!"
(Left) Passengers prepare to board the *Titanic* from the dock at Southampton on the south coast of England. A cutaway reveals some of the ship's staterooms.

(Above) A 1912 poster for the *Titanic* and her nearly identical sister ship, the *Olympic*.

As the group stepped on board the *Titanic*, a man in a blue uniform checked their third-class tickets and directed the Goldsmiths toward a small room near the stern of the ship. Mr. Theobald and Alfred were given berths in tiny rooms near the *Titanic*'s bow.

Several decks above them, twelve-year-old Billy Carter and his family were being shown to their staterooms in the first-class section of the *Titanic*. Billy was happy to be going home to Philadelphia on this brand-new ship. The Carters had been living in England for the past year. Billy and his older sister Lucile had attended boarding schools there. Billy hadn't liked his school very much, but he did like what he had seen so far of the *Titanic*. "She's the world's biggest ship, you know," his father had said to him more than once that morning, "and practically unsinkable, I'm told."

Mr. Carter was bringing a new Renault automobile back to America. It was stowed in the *Titanic*'s hold, not far from where Alfred Rush and Mr. Theobald had their berths. The chauffeur who would drive the car was also on board, staying in the second-class area of the ship.

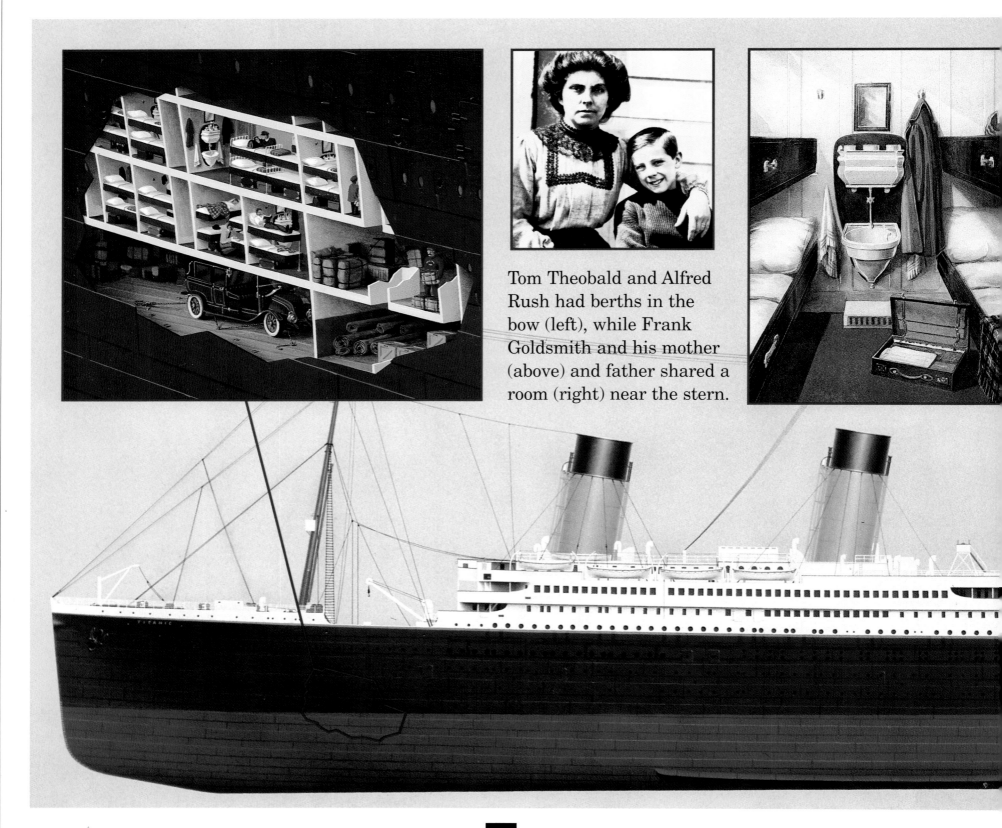

Tom Theobald and Alfred Rush had berths in the bow (left), while Frank Goldsmith and his mother (above) and father shared a room (right) near the stern.

Billy was very happy that the family was keeping their two small dogs in their rooms with them. Other *Titanic* passengers, he had been told, had chosen to place their dogs in the ship's kennel. As his mother was supervising the unpacking of their luggage, Billy decided to take their King Charles spaniel for a walk on the boat deck.

Although it was cool on the open deck, many passengers had gathered there to watch the *Titanic*'s departure. Some of them were waving to friends on the dockside below. Billy walked over to the other side of the ship and saw three tugboats puffing smoke as they prepared to tow

the *Titanic* away from the pier.

Deep inside the ship, Mrs. Goldsmith was carefully putting away her family's belongings in their tiny room. Frank was thrilled to be sleeping in a bunk bed and immediately claimed the upper bunk for himself. In the narrow corridor outside the room, he met two boys about his own age. Soon all three were running up and down stairs and pushing their way through crowded passageways. On the very lowest deck, the boys peered down into the ship's boiler rooms. Frank saw men shoveling coal into the flames of the huge furnaces that powered the *Titanic*'s steam engines. One

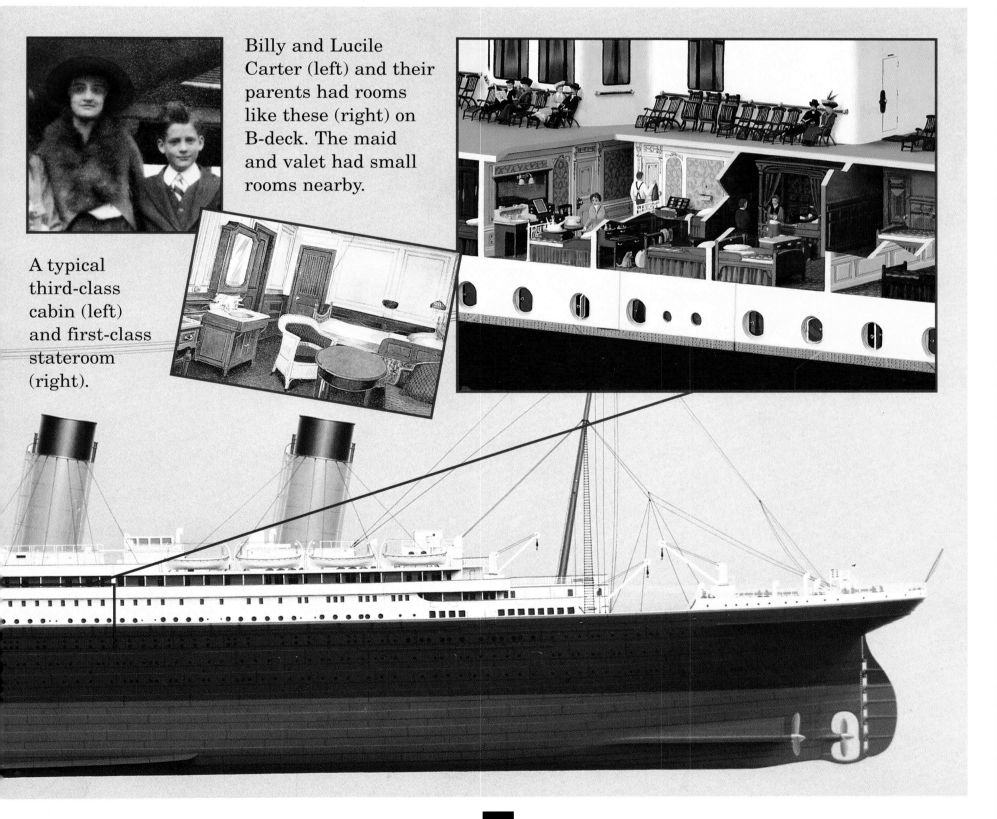

Billy and Lucile Carter (left) and their parents had rooms like these (right) on B-deck. The maid and valet had small rooms nearby.

A typical third-class cabin (left) and first-class stateroom (right).

man with a face black from coal dust put down his shovel and waved at him.

As Frank climbed back upstairs with his new friends, he suddenly saw Alfred Rush. "Frankie!" Alfred called out. "Your ma sent me looking for you! It's time for us to eat." He led Frank back to his family's room. "Here he is, Mrs. Goldsmith. He'd just got lost." Frank could see that his mother was angry with him. But she seemed ready to accept Alfred's excuse. Perhaps Alfred was all right after all, Frank thought.

The first meal of the *Titanic*'s maiden voyage was served later than anyone expected. While moving out of port, the *Titanic* had nearly collided with another ship. Billy Carter saw it all from the boat deck. As the huge *Titanic* moved down the channel, its wake caused a ship moored beside the dock to swing outward right into its path. The ship's stern came closer and closer until there were only inches between it and the *Titanic*. Just when it seemed as if the two ships would crash, a tugboat moved in and quickly pulled the smaller ship away while the *Titanic* reversed its engines. But the delay took more than an hour. As Billy and the other passengers went downstairs for lunch, everyone was talking about the near accident. He heard one man say, "It's not a good start for a maiden voyage, if you ask me."

Frank Goldsmith and his parents joined Mr. Theobald and Alfred Rush at one of the long tables in the third-class dining saloon. The smell of food made Frank realize just how hungry he was. A hearty soup was followed by corned beef and cabbage served with boiled potatoes and all the fresh bread he could eat. Frank thought he had never eaten so well—or so much.

But he could not have imagined the kind of food being served to the Carters in the first-class dining saloon two decks above him. While Billy Carter described to his family what he had seen from the boat deck, uniformed stewards served them course after course from silver trays. Billy was happy to try the fresh lobster, shrimp and roast beef, but left behind the pickled herrings and corned ox tongue. His sister Lucile had spent her morning exploring the *Titanic* and promised to show Billy the ship's gymnasium, Turkish bath and swimming pool after lunch.

The first-class dining saloon
This elegant dining room was where some of the richest passengers on the *Titanic* ate their meals. It was the largest room on any ship and could serve over 500 people at one time.

The kitchens
The chefs who cooked for first- and second-class passengers (above) and for the third-class dining saloon prepared over 4,000 meals a day. Electric potato peelers, vegetable slicers, and ice-cream machines helped make their work easier.

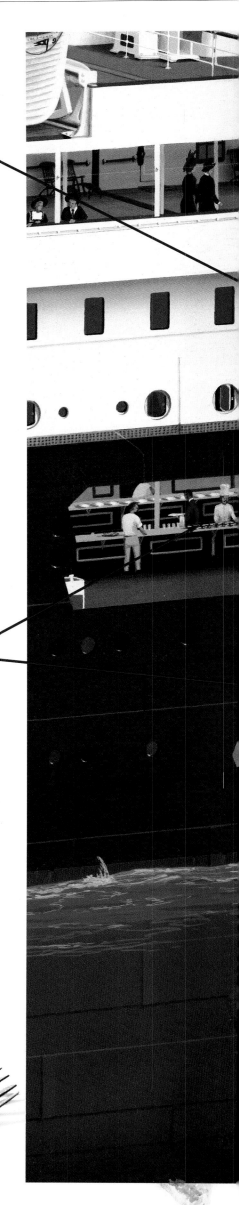

The third-class dining saloon
The dining room for third-class passengers served simple, nourishing meals. It was clean and comfortable with white tablecloths covering the long tables.

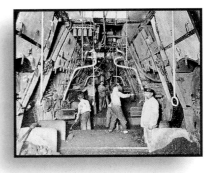

The boiler room
Far below the passengers, stokers worked around the clock in heat and dirt, shoveling coal into the boilers that drove the *Titanic*'s giant steam engines. The fifteen-foot-high boilers are shown below, before they were brought on board the ship.

Gymnasium
The *Titanic*'s gym instructor shows how to use the rowing machine (above).

First-class Promenade
This deck was a favorite place for children of first-class passengers to play.

First-class dining saloon
Here waiters served many fancy dishes, but a steward (above) would also serve hot drinks on deck.

The Grand Staircase

Billy and Lucile go down the elegant staircase, which had a large glass dome overhead to let the sunlight shine through.

No. 659

WHITE STAR LINE.

R.M.S. "TITANIC."

This ticket entitles bearer to use of Turkish or Electric Bath on one occasion.

Paid 4/= or 1 Dollar.

Turkish Baths

After a steam bath, *Titanic* passengers could cool off in a room decorated like a Turkish palace. Then they often went next door for a dip in the ship's swimming pool (below).

TITANIC

Length:
882 1/2 feet
(269 meters)

Width:
92 1/2 feet
(28 meters)

Top speed:
24 knots

Coal carried:
5,892 tons (5,344
metric tons)

**Maximum
capacity of the
Titanic:**
3,547 people

**Passengers and
crew aboard April
14, 1912:**
Approx. 2,222 people

Lifeboats:
16, plus
4 collapsibles,
total capacity
1,178 people

Poop deck

Third-class
general room

Third-cla
cabins

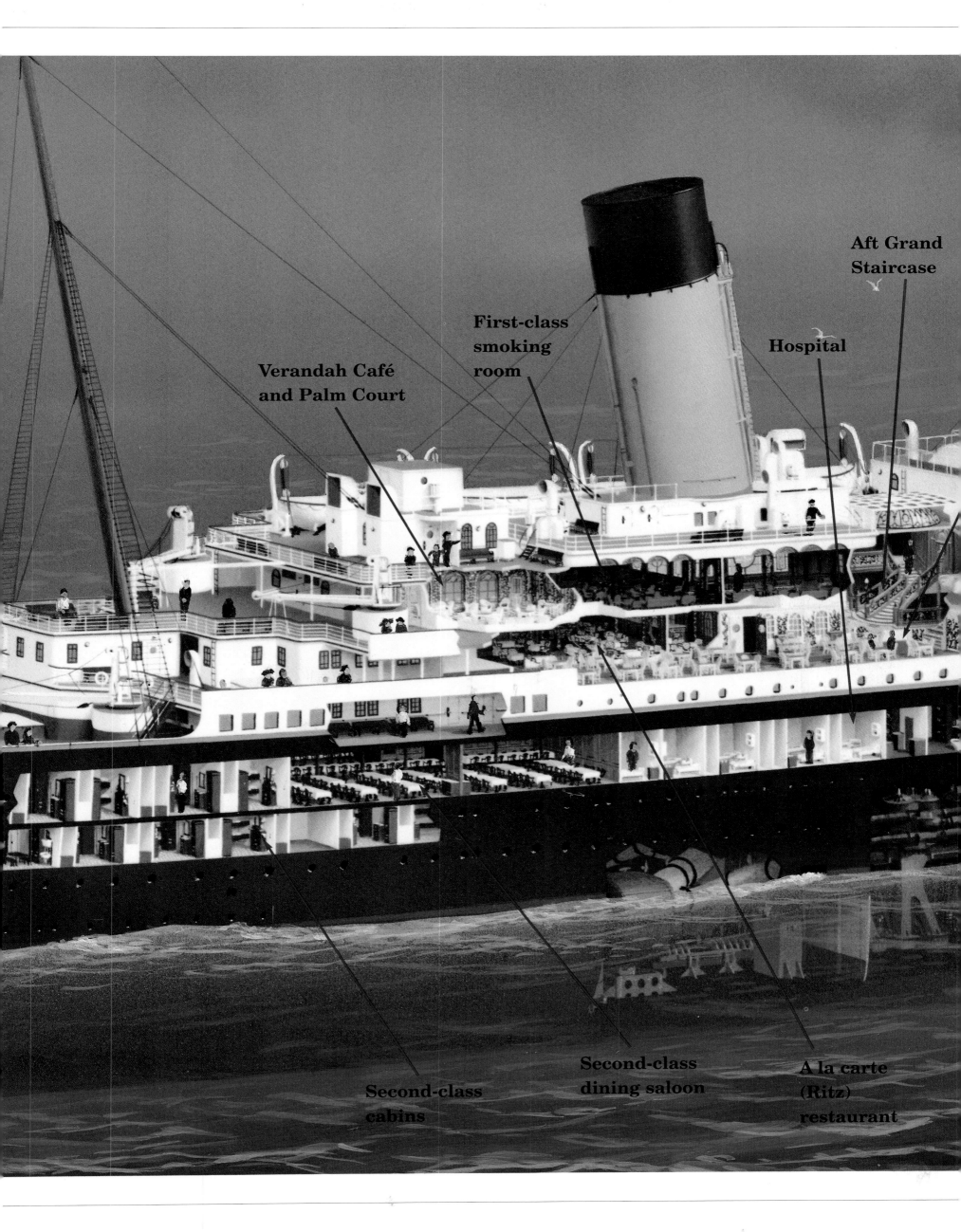

Aft Grand
Staircase

First-class
smoking
room

Hospital

Verandah Café
and Palm Court

Second-class
cabins

Second-class
dining saloon

A la carte
(Ritz)
restaurant

Café Parisien

First-class staterooms

Compass platform

Whistles

First-class lounge

First-class dining saloon

Gymnasium

Wireless room

Grand Staircase

First-class promenade

Boiler room

Third-class dining saloon

First-class reception room

Engine room

Wheelhouse

Bridge

Crow's nest

Private
deck for
deluxe
suite

Turkish
baths

Swimming
pool

Third-class
berths

A Quiet Sunday

Sunday, April 14, 1912

By the fifth day of the *Titanic*'s voyage, Frank Goldsmith and his friends had explored every part of the ship open to boys in third class. They loved to climb on the huge cranes in the well deck that moved baggage into the *Titanic*'s holds. One of the boys had dared Frank to swing hand over hand from a wire cable under a crane. By the time he climbed down, his hands were covered with oily grease. His mother had to scrub them several times before it all came off.

On Sunday morning, Frank and his mother attended a church service. Afterward, they went for a walk on the

stern deck. Although it was very cold, many passengers were outside enjoying the bright sunshine and the calm ocean. Alfred Rush came running up to Frank and his mother. "Look, Mrs. Goldsmith! I've got a birthday present!" He opened his hand to show them a sixpence coin. He explained that he had been given a refund on the amount paid in advance to store his baggage on the ship.

"A birthday present?" Frank asked. "Is it really your birthday?"

"Why yes, Frankie," Alfred replied. "I'm sixteen today. Look, I'm wearing my long trousers." In his new trousers, Alfred felt like a man. Frank glanced down at his own short pants. He looked forward to the day when he would be sixteen and could wear long trousers, too.

Later that afternoon, Billy and Lucile Carter decided to walk their two small dogs on the upper deck. As they approached the rear of the deck, Billy pointed down toward the stern. "Oh, look, Lucy, they're walking the dogs from the kennel." Below them on the stern deck, a crewman was walking in a large circle with three dog leashes in each hand.

By the time Lucile and Billy left the boat deck, the sky was turning pink. As they returned to their room, Billy wondered whether they should tell their parents to come and see the beautiful sunset. Lucile quickly reminded him that they would be busy dressing for dinner. Mr. and Mrs. Carter were to attend a dinner party for Captain Smith in the *Titanic*'s Ritz restaurant that evening. "So it will be just you and me at our table tonight, Billy," she said.

Sunday on the Stern Decks

From the upper deck, Billy and Lucile Carter could see a member of the crew walking the dogs of the first-class passengers.

The cranes on the well deck were used at the beginning of the voyage to move cargo into the ship.

Frank Goldsmith and his mother enjoy a stroll on the poop deck.

Other passengers chose to spend the afternoon in the third-class general room, where they could read, write letters or chat with friends and family.

The bridge
The *Titanic*'s bridge was the control center for the ship. On the day of the disaster, the *Titanic* received many warnings that icebergs lay ahead. But that night Captain Smith (below) left his officers in charge of guiding the ship's course.

"Iceberg right ahead!"
When lookout Frederick Fleet spotted the iceberg at 11:40 P.M., he quickly telephoned the bridge to report what he had seen.

"Full speed astern!"
As soon as he heard Fleet's report, First Officer William Murdoch ran to the telegraph that sent messages to the engine room and ordered the engines to be reversed.

"Hard a' starboard!"
Murdoch then ordered the ship's wheel (above) to be turned hard a' starboard to avoid the iceberg.

To the Lifeboats

Sunday, April 14, 1912, 11:40 P.M.

Late on Sunday evening, Mr. Carter was in the *Titanic*'s first-class smoking room. He and some of the men who had attended the dinner for Captain Smith were enjoying a final cigar before bedtime. Suddenly they felt a jolt and heard a strange grinding noise. A few of the men ran out on deck and Mr. Carter quickly followed them. He heard a voice call out, "We hit an iceberg — there it is!" Behind the ship he could just make out a dark shape against the starlit sky. As he hurried downstairs, he noticed how quiet it was. The noise of the ship's engines had stopped. Finding that his family were all in bed, he told his wife that she should wake the children. Mrs. Carter woke Billy and Lucile and told them to get dressed quickly.

At about this time, Frank Goldsmith's father woke up. He quickly noticed that the throbbing of the ship's engines had stopped. Mr. Goldsmith decided to dress and go outside to find out why the ship was not moving. When he returned, he told his wife that the *Titanic* had hit an iceberg but she should not worry about it. "You can dress Frankie if you want to," he added. As Frank's mother helped her sleepy son into his clothes, a crewman knocked on their door and told them to put on life jackets. He said they might have to get into a lifeboat and go away from the ship for a while. Frank was now fully awake. Going into a lifeboat! That sounded exciting.

Frank and his mother put on their life jackets while Mr. Goldsmith packed a small suitcase. Outside their room, Mr. Theobald and Alfred Rush were waiting. Together they walked upstairs to the second-class area. There they were told that no luggage could be taken up to the boat deck, so Mr. Goldsmith left the suitcase behind. Up another flight of stairs, the group came to a gateway where a crewman was standing guard. He told them that only women and children were allowed through to get into the lifeboats. Mr. Goldsmith put his arm around Frank's mother. He then reached down, hugged Frank's shoulders and said, "So long, Frankie, I'll see you later."

Mr. Theobald took off his wedding ring and gave it to Mrs. Goldsmith. "If I don't see you in New York," he said, "will you see that my wife gets this?" Frank wondered why he looked so serious. They were just going into the lifeboat for a little while, weren't they? Frank's mother put the ring on her finger and took Frank through the gateway. Then the crewman reached out to pull Alfred Rush through the gate to the lifeboats. But Alfred jerked his arm out of the sailor's hand. "No!" he said firmly. "I'm staying here with the men!"

On the other side of the boat deck, Billy Carter, his mother and sister had been waiting for more than an hour to get into Lifeboat No. 4. While they waited, the deck beneath their feet began to tilt downward as the *Titanic*'s bow sank deeper in the water. All but a few of the *Titanic*'s lifeboats had already left, but most of her passengers and crew were still on board. People were now beginning to realize that the *Titanic* was actually going to sink. But there were no signs of panic from the people standing near Billy on the boat deck. Sometimes they could hear parts of the lively tunes being played on deck by the ship's band.

When the loading of Lifeboat No. 4 finally began, an officer noticed a teenage boy about to enter. "That boy can't go!" he said, putting out his hand.

"Of course that boy goes with his mother," his father protested. "He is only thirteen!"

The officer gave in, saying, "Very well, but no more boys!"

Hearing this, Mrs. Carter took off her hat and placed it on Billy's head. There were no objections from anyone when Billy, his sister, mother and mother's maid were helped into the lifeboat. As the boat was lowered past lighted rooms, Billy could see water swirling around the elegant furniture inside. He wondered if his father would manage to escape from the sinking ship.

Mr. Carter had left his family at Lifeboat No. 4 over an hour before. He did not know that there had been a delay in lowering it. By the time Lifeboat No. 4 was finally lowered at around 1:55 A.M., Mr. Carter

As the *Titanic* sank
Here the *Titanic* is shown as it looked at about 1:35 A.M., though events that occurred before and after this time are also depicted.

1) 12:15 A.M.
The band plays waltzes and popular songs on the deck until just before 2 A.M.

2) 1:10 A.M.
Rockets are fired from the bridge to attract the attention of any nearby ships.

3) 1:35 A.M.
Lifeboat No. 15 is nearly lowered on top of boat No. 13. At the last moment, crewmen in No. 13 manage to row their boat out of the way.

4) 1:55 A.M.
Lifeboat No. 4 is launched. It carries Billy Carter, his sister, his mother, his mother's maid and thirty-two other women and children.

5) 2:00 A.M.
Collapsible C is launched from the *Titanic* with thirty-nine people on board, including Frank Goldsmith, his mother and Mr. Carter.

was on the other side of the boat deck, helping to load passengers into one of the emergency boats. These were extra lifeboats with collapsible canvas sides. No one had thought these boats would ever have to be used on the brand-new "unsinkable" *Titanic*. But even the emergency boats could carry only a small number of the many people still on board.

Frank Goldsmith and his mother found seats in the front of Collapsible Lifeboat C. This was the same boat that Mr. Carter was helping to load. When some men tried to climb into the boat, the officer in charge fired his pistol in the air and ordered them out. Collapsible C was then filled with women and children. Just as the sailors were starting to lower the boat to the water, Mr. Carter saw that there was some space left. He could see no other women or children waiting, so he stepped in. The sinking *Titanic* was tilting so far to one side that as the lifeboat was lowered, its canvas sides rubbed against the rivets in the *Titanic*'s hull. Mrs. Goldsmith and the other passengers had to push the lifeboat away from the hull with their hands to allow it to continue down to the water.

When Collapsible C landed in the calm, dark ocean, the crewmen on board began rowing it away from the ship. Frank could see that the *Titanic*'s bow was almost completely underwater, yet its lights still gleamed against the night sky. He could see many people clustered on the *Titanic*'s stern, but he did not know that there were still over 1,500 left on the ship with little chance of escape.

Suddenly the *Titanic* lurched forward and its stern was lifted even higher out of the water. Then all the lights on the ship went out and Frank heard what sounded like explosions and the shouts of people falling into the water. His mother pressed his head against her chest, but Frank could still hear the sounds of wailing voices. Hundreds of people were crying out in the freezing water.

Someone in the lifeboat exclaimed, "Oh, look, it's going to float!" Frank's mother opened her arms and he turned to see the stern of the *Titanic* aimed almost straight up toward the stars. The ship seemed to stay that way for several minutes. Then it slowly began to sink. Many people wept as the *Titanic* finally vanished under the black water.

Saying farewell
On the boat deck (above) wives say goodbye to their husbands. By 2 A.M. Lifeboat No. 4 (right) has reached the water. Inside the *Titanic*, sheets and towels float in the flooded storerooms and water rises up the Grand Staircase.

In the lifeboats
The White Star flag (above) was attached to every lifeboat. (Below) A life jacket worn by one of the *Titanic*'s passengers.

How the *Titanic* sank

It took about three hours for the "unsinkable" ship to fill with water, break in two and plunge to the bottom of the ocean.

1) The front of the ship, nearest to where the iceberg hit, was the first section to go under.

2) As the bow sank deeper, the stern rose until it was standing almost straight up.

3) People in the lifeboats heard a sound as loud as an explosion when the *Titanic* broke apart between its third and fourth funnels (right).

4) The bow section sank first. The stern slowly filled with water, then followed the bow to the ocean floor a few minutes later.

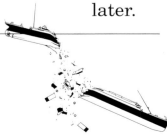

Rescue

Monday, April 15, 4:30 A.M.

hroughout the cold, dark night, the passengers in the *Titanic*'s lifeboats waited and prayed for rescue. Billy Carter's mother helped row Lifeboat No. 4. In Collapsible C, Frank Goldsmith's mother gave up her straw hat to be set on fire to attract the attention of any passing ships. Frank eventually fell asleep in her arms. When he awoke, the sky was getting lighter, and he saw that their lifeboat was being rowed toward a ship. It was the R.M.S. *Carpathia*. The captain of the *Carpathia* had heard the *Titanic*'s SOS radio call and had raced to the scene of the disaster. By the time he arrived, all that remained of the *Titanic* were its lifeboats bobbing on the waves.

Frank was hauled up the side of the *Carpathia* in a sling, and his mother followed him on a rope ladder. On reaching the deck, they were given hot drinks and blankets. Mr. Carter, who had also been in Collapsible C, watched anxiously as other boats came alongside the

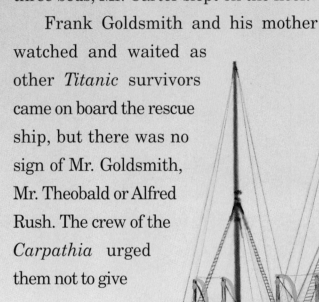

Carpathia. When Lifeboat No. 4 came near, he caught sight of his wife and daughter. "Where's my son?" he called out, leaning over the railing. "Where's my son?"

Billy Carter, still wearing his mother's hat, lifted the brim and cried out, "Here I am, Father, here I am!" The Carters were reunited on the deck of the *Carpathia* and given a small, private room. Since it only had three beds, Mr. Carter slept on the floor.

Frank Goldsmith and his mother watched and waited as other *Titanic* survivors came on board the rescue ship, but there was no sign of Mr. Goldsmith, Mr. Theobald or Alfred Rush. The crew of the *Carpathia* urged them not to give

up hope. Perhaps some *Titanic* passengers had been picked up by other boats. Mrs. Goldsmith decided to spend her time helping to make emergency clothes out of blankets for other rescued passengers. Many of them had escaped from the *Titanic* wearing only pajamas or nightgowns.

Several of the surviving crewmen from the *Titanic* offered to help look after the rescued children. Frank

soon found himself taking a walk around the *Carpathia* with a man named Sam Collins. He realized that Sam was one of the stokers from the *Titanic*'s boiler rooms. Frank and his friends had enjoyed seeing them sing and beat time with their shovels as they worked. Over the next three days, Frank spent many hours with Sam and a group of other crewmen from the *Titanic*, listening to stories of their adventures on board ships.

On the evening of April 18, Frank was sitting with Sam in the crew's dining room on the *Carpathia*. Suddenly he saw a light glide past the porthole. "Oh, that ship nearly hit us," he cried out.

"That was a harbor light, not a ship, Frankie," Sam replied. "We're in New York harbor. We'll soon be docking!" When they went up on deck, newspaper reporters in small boats were calling out questions to people on the decks of the *Carpathia*. The dockside was crowded. The whole world wanted to know how a brand-new "unsinkable" ship could have gone down with such a terrible loss of life. Of the more than 2,200 people on board, only 705 were saved.

When they arrived in New York, Frank and Mrs. Goldsmith were taken care of by the Salvation Army. There they finally realized that there was no hope of ever seeing Frank's father again. Mr. Goldsmith, along with Mr. Theobald, Alfred Rush, Frank's playmates on the ship and more than 1,500 other people, had died when the *Titanic* sank.

Frank and his mother were given new clothes and train tickets to Detroit, where Mrs. Goldsmith's sister lived.

Although they missed his father, Frank and his mother decided to stay on in Detroit and make Mr. Goldsmith's dream of a new life in the United States come true. Frank went to school and grew up like any other American boy. Sometimes Sam Collins kept in touch by letter. When Frank turned sixteen, he got his first pair of long trousers, and thought of Alfred Rush, who had died on the *Titanic* on his sixteenth birthday.

As a man, Frank married and had three sons of his own.

When he was older, he wrote a book about his experiences on the *Titanic*. Frank Goldsmith died in 1982 and his ashes were scattered on the ocean in the place where the *Titanic* sank and he had lost his father.

After leaving the *Carpathia*, Billy Carter's family went back home to Philadelphia. Billy grew up and became a successful Philadelphia businessman. He died there in 1985. In September of that same year, the wreck of the *Titanic* was found more than two miles beneath the sea by an American/French exploration team headed by Dr. Robert Ballard. For the first time in more than seventy years, the world was able to look again at the great liner, now lying in two pieces on the ocean floor.

We do not know if Billy Carter saw photographs of the eerie wreck. Throughout his life, Billy never liked to speak about the *Titanic*. Like many *Titanic* survivors, he tried to forget that cold, clear night in 1912 when the R.M.S. *Titanic* went to its grave.

Exploring the wreck

Dr. Robert Ballard (below) climbs into his submarine *Alvin* in July of 1986. The lights from *Alvin* (left) shine on the bow of the sunken liner.

The bow and stern sections of the wreck (below) lie 1,970 feet apart. Inside what was once the Grand Staircase (right), an underwater robot shines its beam on a dangling light fixture.

Glossary

A-deck, B-deck: The *Titanic*'s passenger decks were given the letters A through G. A-deck was the first deck below the boat deck.

berths: Single beds within a shared room.

boat deck: The deck of a ship on which the lifeboats are carried. On the *Titanic*, this was the top deck.

boiler: A furnace in which coal was burned to boil water and create steam, which in turn drove the ship.

bow: The front end of a ship.

bridge: A raised platform or structure toward the front end of a ship, which has a clear view ahead, and from which the ship is navigated.

crow's nest: A lookout platform high on a ship's mast.

funnel: A tall smokestack on a ship.

gangway: A ramp that allowed passengers to walk from the dock onto the ship.

hold: A storage space for cargo on a ship, usually below decks.

hull: The frame or lower body of a ship that is partly below water when it is sailing.

maiden voyage: The first voyage of a ship.

passageway: A corridor on a ship.

poop deck: The high deck at the stern of a ship.

port: The left-hand side of a ship when facing the bow.

promenade: An upper deck, sometimes enclosed, on which passengers could stroll.

Ritz restaurant: A name passengers used to refer to the *Titanic*'s elegant first-class restaurant, which was decorated to look like the Ritz Hotel in London.

rockets: The *Titanic* fired flares that were like fireworks as a sign that it was in distress.

starboard: The right-hand side of a ship when facing the bow.

stern: The rear end of a ship.

steward: A member of a ship's crew who attends to the needs of passengers and to the food supplies.

stoker: A crew member who keeps a ship's boilers working to drive the engines.

surviving crewmen: Sam Collins and some of the other men of the *Titanic*'s crew survived because they were put into lifeboats to handle the oars.

survivors: 705 people survived the *Titanic* disaster. Over 1,500 people died. The precise number of victims is unknown because there are no exact records of everyone on board.

telegraph: A circular machine with a rotating handle that sent messages from the *Titanic*'s bridge to its engine rooms.

Turkish bath: A steam bath.

White Star Line: The company that owned the *Titanic* and her sister ship, the *Olympic*.

wireless: An early form of radio.

Photograph and Illustration Credits

Every effort has been made to correctly attribute all the material reproduced in this book. If any errors have unwittingly occurred, we will be happy to correct them in future editions.

All illustrations, unless otherwise designated, are by Ken Marschall © 1997.

Page 5: Private Collection
Page 6: (all) Titanic Historical Society
Page 7: (left) Lucy Trowbridge Collection; (right) Ken Marschall Collection
Page 8: (top, middle) Ken Marschall Collection; (bottom) Private Collection
Page 9: (top) Ken Marschall Collection; (middle) Ken Marschall Collection; (bottom) Harland & Wolff

Page 10: (top) The Father Browne S.J. Collection; (middle) The Father Browne S.J. Collection/Ken Marschall Collection; (bottom) Titanic Historical Society
Page 11: (top) Library of Congress/Ken Marschall Collection; (middle) George Behe Collection; (bottom) *Illustrated London News*
Page 17: Ulster Folk & Transport Museum, Northern Ireland
Page 18: *Illustrated London News*
Page 19: Bill Sauder Collection
Pages 22-23: Peter Kovalik/Ken Marschall
Page 24: (top) The Mariner's Museum; (middle) Private Collection; (bottom) Titanic Historical Society
Page 31: (middle) Perry Thorvsvik © National Geographic Society

Recommended Further Reading

On Board the Titanic
by Shelley Tanaka
Paintings by Ken Marschall, 1996
(*Hyperion, U.S.; Scholastic, Canada*)
Paintings and diagrams illustrate the true stories of how seventeen-year-old Jack Thayer and junior radio operator Harold Bride survived the sinking of the *Titanic*.

Polar the Titanic Bear
by Daisy Corning Stone Spedden
Illustrated by Laurie McGaw, 1994
(*Little, Brown and Company, U.S., Canada, U.K.*)
Told through the eyes of a young boy's toy bear, this is the true story of a family's travels, including their voyage on the *Titanic*.

Exploring the Titanic
by Robert D. Ballard, 1988
(*Scholastic, U.S. and U.K.; Penguin, Canada*)
The exciting story of the *Titanic*'s sinking and how it was discovered in 1985 on the ocean floor.

Titanic: An Illustrated History
by Don Lynch and Ken Marschall, 1992
(*Hyperion, U.S.; Penguin, Canada; Hodder and Stoughton, U.K.*)
A richly illustrated, in-depth account of the *Titanic* and the people who sailed on it. (Adult reading level)

Echoes in the Night: Memories of a Titanic Survivor
by Frank J.W. Goldsmith, 1991
(*A Titanic Historical Society, Inc. Publication., U.S.*)
Frank Goldsmith's own account of what it was like to sail on the great liner.

Acknowledgments

Madison Press Books would like to thank the following for their generous assistance: Don Lynch; Alison Reid; Darrell Rooney; Charles Chafee; George Behe; Bill Sauder; the Titanic Historical Society. For more information about membership in the Titanic Historical Society, please write *Titanic Historical Society*, P.O. Box 51053, Indian Orchard, Massachusetts, 01151-0053, U.S.A.

Prints and posters of Ken Marschall's work are available from *Trans-Atlantic Designs*, P.O. Box 820376, Houston, Texas, U.S.A. 77282-0376